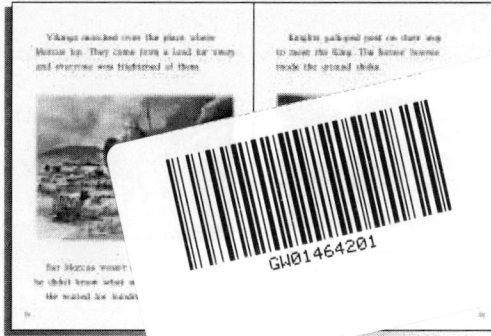

**CHECK** for *Vikings*.

"Look at the first letter, and then try to find a little word you know."

"The Vikings were people from another country who came to Britain when they explored the seas."

**CHECK** for *Knights*.

"The *k* in this word is silent. Can you read the rest of the word? Knights were the king's soldiers."

**Pages 12–13**

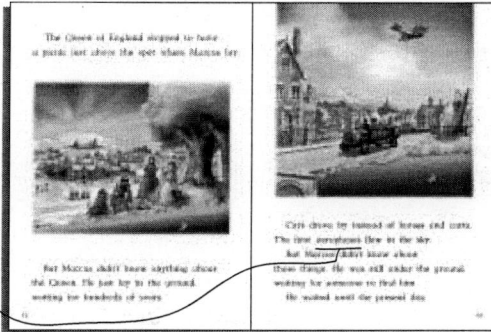

**aeroplanes**
"Leave a gap, read on and reread from the start of the sentence. Search the picture for further clues and think what would make sense."

Ask the child to read on to the end of the story, checking that he or she reads with pace and pays attention to the punctuation, especially the commas.

Spend a few moments concentrating on the time line on page 16 as a group. Suggestions for working on this page are given overleaf.

## After Independent Reading/Returning to the text

**Word knowledge – discriminate syllables within multi-syllabic words**

Write the names of characters on the flipchart (*Marcus*, *Julia*, *Vikings*, and *Tim*).

Ask the children to clap the syllables in each name. Then tell them to listen while you clap one of the names, and to put their hands up when the number of syllables in the clapped name matches the number of syllables in their own name. Ask each child to clap the syllables in his or her own name. Extend by clapping the names of other children in the class and asking the group to guess them.

**Sentence knowledge – read aloud with intonation and expression appropriate to the grammar**

Read page 12 aloud, this time concentrating on phrasing within extended sentences. Focus on the first sentence and look at the way the phrases expand the central idea (*the Queen … stopped*).

**Text knowledge – retell the story in sequence, using key words and phrases from the text**

Ask each child in the group to recount one incident that happened while Marcus was underground. Write them on the flipchart and ask the children to place them in order. Start to retell the story, using words and phrases from the text. Ask individual children to continue the narrative, using the prompts on the flipchart. Read the last page together and check that the sequence of events constructed by the children matches the time line.

## Responding to the text

- Ask the children who made the clay dog.
- Can they remember what happened to Marcus?
- How many years do they think passed by before Tim found Marcus?
- Discuss what the children know about Roman Britain, the Vikings, or early 20th century Britain. Would they like to have been alive then?

# How to use these notes

## Guided Reading

### Walkthrough/Book introduction *(pages 2–3)*

A *walkthrough*, or book introduction, is a way of introducing the book to a group of children. During the walkthrough, children are introduced to some of the ideas and significant vocabulary they will meet when they read the book.

Go through the whole of the walkthrough before the children start reading independently. The walkthrough notes on pages 2 and 3 of this booklet provide prompts for you to use, specific to *The Clay Dog*. The questions, comments and suggestions alert children to ideas and vocabulary they will need in order to read independently and with full understanding.

### Independent Reading *(pages 4–5)*

After doing a walkthrough, ask the children to read the text aloud, on their own, at their own pace. Observe the strategies each child uses, praising successful problem solving and expressive reading. Prompts are suggested for good phrasing, use of word-solving skills, predicting and checking the meaning, and actively monitoring the implications of the text, on pages 4 and 5.

### After Independent Reading/ Returning to the text *(page 6)*

After the children have read the book independently, return to the text as a group to reinforce teaching points and to check children's understanding. On page 6, there are quick follow-up ideas for related text, sentence and word level work.

### Responding to the text *(pages 6–8)*

It is important to encourage children to give a personal response to the text. Discussion ideas related to the book are on page 6.

These Teaching Notes also contain group activity ideas on page 7, and a Photocopy Master on page 8, for use after the guided reading session or in a follow-up literacy session.

# Guided Reading Notes

## Walkthrough

Explain to the group that this story is about a toy dog that was lost nearly 2000 years ago. It's called *The Clay Dog*. Ask the children to read the back cover blurb. What might this story tell us about the past?

### Pages 2–3

**PROMPTS** When do you think the story is set? What do the pictures tell us? Do you recognize the style of clothes the people are wearing? (Prompt for *Roman times*.)

The little girl is called Julia, and her clay dog is called Marcus. Can you find their names in the text? Look for the first letters J and M.

Long, long ago, Julia found some clay
in her father's workshop.
"Please will you make something for me?"
she asked.

Her father made the clay into the shape
of a dog. Then he baked it hard and dry.
"I think I'll call him Marcus," said Julia,
as she took him with her to play.

Walk through the book to page 8 with the children, asking them to say what's happening in the story by looking at the pictures. Make sure that they understand that Marcus has been lost.

### Pages 8–9

**PROMPTS** Marcus was waiting for someone to find him. He waited for a very long time. How do the pictures show that he's been waiting for a long time? (Prompt for *the mud and grass cover him*.)

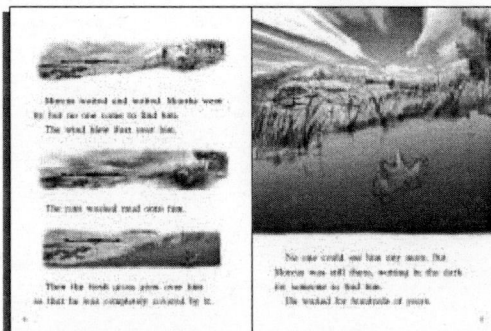

Marcus waited and waited. Months went
by but no one came to find him.
The wind blew dust over him.

The rain washed mud onto him.

Then the fresh grass grew over him
so that he was completely covered by it.

No one could see him any more, but
Marcus was still there, waiting in the dark
for someone to find him.
He waited for hundreds of years.

2

## Pages 10–11

**PROMPTS** Whilst Marcus lay under the ground, hundreds of years went by. Different people passed above where he lay. Do you think these people found Marcus? No, he just went on lying there, waiting and waiting to be found.

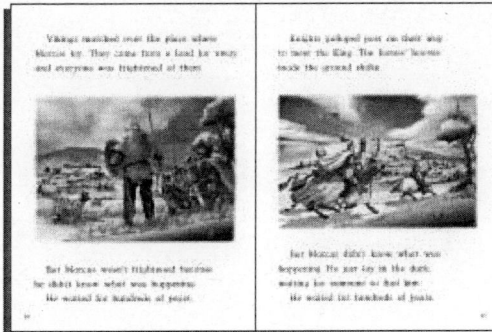

## Pages 12–13

**PROMPTS** More people passed over Marcus. What are they doing? Has Marcus been under the ground for a very long time? How can you tell? (Prompt for *the old-fashioned car and aeroplane in the picture*.)

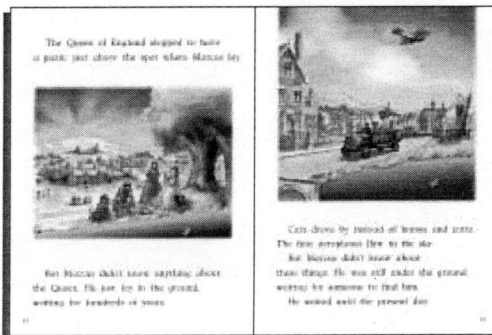

Continue the walkthrough to page 16, discussing the illustrations.

## Page 16

**PROMPTS** This page shows us how long Marcus was under the ground. The numbers tell us the dates when the different people went past. (If necessary, explain that AD means *Anno Domini*, and is a way of writing down dates.)

Tell the children that you'll come back to this page once they've read the story.

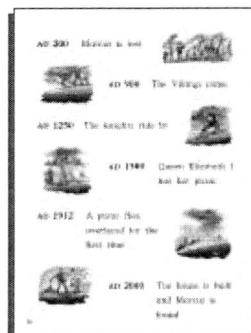

Tell the children to read the book independently up to page 15. (Page 16 will be discussed after independent reading.) Encourage them to jot down people who passed by and incidents that occurred above the spot where Marcus lay.

Remind the children in the group about the range of strategies they can use to work out words if they get stuck. The pictures in *The Clay Dog* will give some clues, but the children will also need to work on the words themselves – by, for example, splitting multi-syllabic and compound words into component parts.

**Pages 4–5**

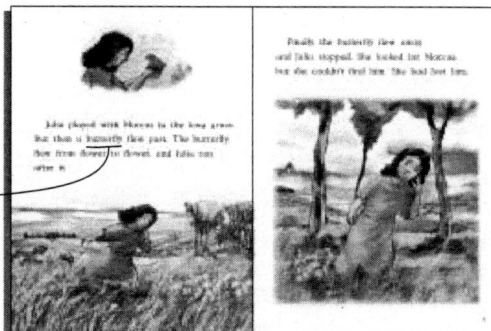

**butterfly**
"Split the compound word into two smaller words."

**CHECK** that the child is checking meaning to read *flower*.
"Where did the butterfly fly?"

**CHECK** that the child understands the use of the apostrophe in *couldn't*.
"The apostrophe tells us that there's a missing letter. Split the word into two (could/n't) and think what would make sense."

Ask the child to read on, checking that he or she reads the contracted words *couldn't*, *I'm*, *don't* and *didn't* fluently.

**Pages 8–9**

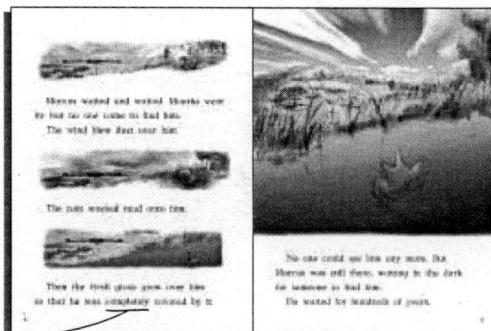

**completely**
"Read the first syllable (com) and blend through the rest of the word."

**CHECK** that the child cross-references pictures and text to follow what's happening in the story.
"What's happened to Marcus? Where is he?" *or* "Well done, you noticed that Marcus has been lost for a long time, and now he's under the ground."

# ❶ Compound word pairs

**AIM** to identify compound words from their component parts
(*NLS: Y2 T2 W4*)

**YOU WILL NEED**
● 14 small pieces of card (playing card size)
● marker pen

**WHAT TO DO** Write the component parts of the compound words from the text
onto the cards: *work, shop, some, thing, butter, fly, for, ever, in, doors,
some, one, work, men.*

Place the cards face down on the table. Explain to the children that
the object of the game is to pick 2 cards and put the two parts
together to see if they make a compound word. Children should take
turns to pick two cards from the table. If the cards make a
compound word, they keep the pair. If they do not, both cards are
returned face down on the table. Children should be encouraged to
remember where each card is placed. The winner of the game is the
player with most pairs.

# ❷ Write a story

**AIM** to use the story setting to write own story; to find words and
phrases that link sentences (*NLS: Y2 T2 T13; Y2 T1 S2*)

**YOU WILL NEED**
● flip chart and pen
● paper and pens/pencils

**WHAT TO DO** Discuss the story setting with the children. Ask them to think about
other events that could have taken place while Marcus lay under the
ground. Write their ideas on the flipchart.

Now draw their attention to the key linking phrases in the text, e.g.
*Long, long ago; Marcus lay in the dark waiting; But Marcus didn't
know what was happening; Months went by; He waited for hundreds
of years.*

Write these up on the flipchart. Ask the children to use their ideas to
write their own story about what happened while Marcus was
underground. They should include some of the linking phrases you
have listed.

Marcus lay under the ground for hundreds of years.
Write down what happened.

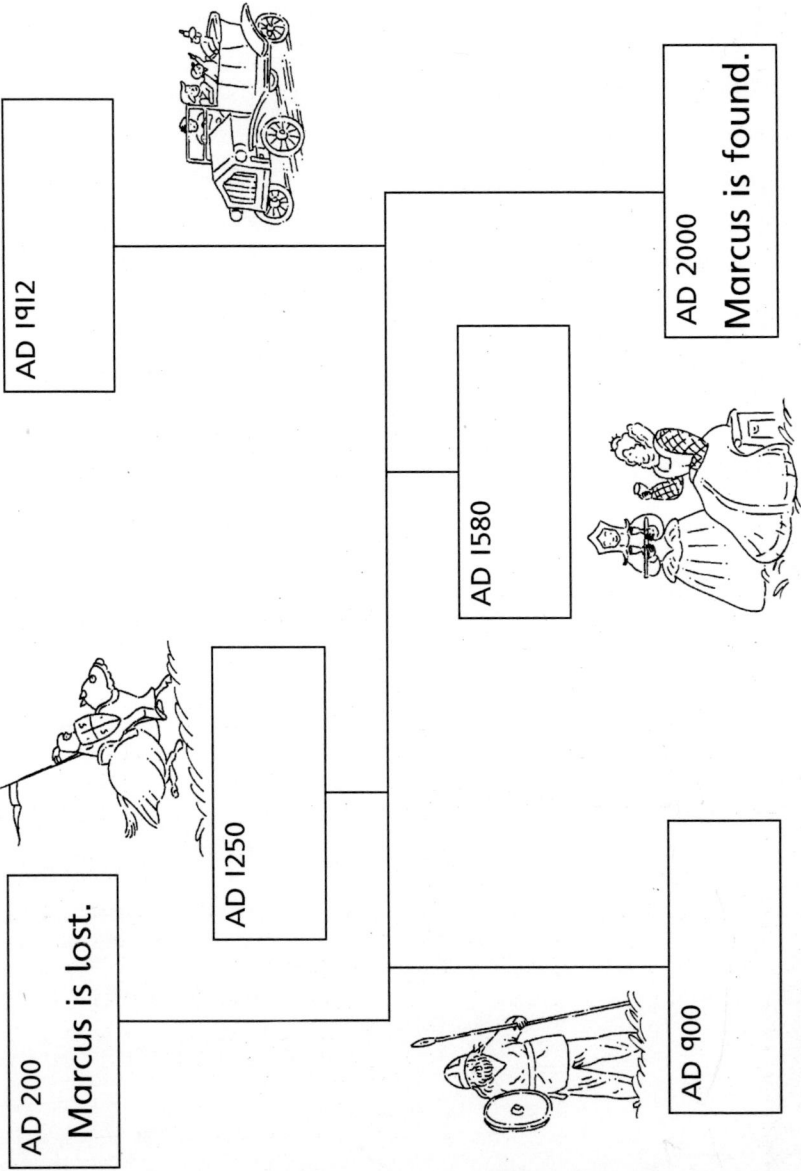

AD 1912

AD 2000 **Marcus is found.**

AD 1580

AD 1250

AD 200 **Marcus is lost.**

AD 900

Children should refer to pages 10-13 in the book to help them complete the time line.
They should then check their time line against the one on page 16 of the book.

**The Clay Dog**                    *(NLS: Y2 T1 T4)*